D.J. and the ZULU PARADE

By Denise Walter McConduit

D.J. and the ZULU PARADE

Illustrated by Emile F. Henriquez
and Lucien C. Barbarin, Jr.

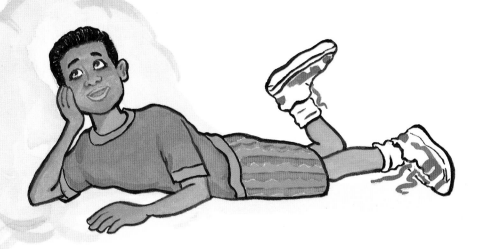

PELICAN PUBLISHING COMPANY
Gretna 1995

*To my parents, Rene J. Walter and Baylissa C. Walter—
thanks for a wonderful childhood*

---

*The word "Pelican" and the depiction of a pelican are trademarks
of Pelican Publishing Company, Inc.,
and are registered in the U.S. Patent and Trademark Office.*

Library of Congress Cataloging-in-Publication Data

McConduit, Denise Walter.
    D.J. and the Zulu parade / Denise Walter McConduit ; illustrated
by Emile F. Henriquez and Lucien C. Barbarin, Jr.
      p. cm.
    Summary: On Mardi Gras seven-year-old D.J. experiences the
excitement of being a page to the queen in the Zulu parade, the
oldest black parade in New Orleans.
    ISBN 1-56554-063-8
    [1. Carnival—Fiction. 2. New Orleans (La.)—Fiction.
3. Parades—Fiction. 4. Afro-Americans—Fiction.]   I. Henriquez,
Emile F., ill. II. Barbarin, Lucien C., ill. III. Title.
PZ7.M478414196DaC 1995
[E]—dc20   94-12210
                                                                              CIP
                                                                               AC

Manufactured in China
Published by Pelican Publishing Company, Inc.
1101 Monroe Street, Gretna, Louisiana 70053

D.J. AND THE ZULU PARADE

One day, when I was in the kitchen doing homework, Mom asked, "D.J., how would you like to be a page in the Zulu parade? Mrs. Simms called and said she needed another boy your age to ride with her on the queen's float. Of course, I told her you would love to, because it's such an honor. Just think, my D.J., riding in the Zulu parade on Mardi Gras Day. Oh, I have to tell your grandparents, your sisters, your nannie, and . . ."

"But I've never been on a float before," I interrupted, "and what is a page, anyway?" I knew that Mom had already made my decision. The only problem is that when Mom gets excited, she makes a big deal out of everything.

"D.J., pages are children selected to attend the king or queen on the floats. Some pages wear prince costumes with a cape, and a hat with a feather on it. We all know how you love costumes!"

"Which parade is Zulu?" I asked. "Is it that African parade?"

"Not exactly," said Mom. "The people in the parade are from New Orleans, like us. Your Uncle Pete is riding in the parade this year. The Zulus started parading around 1910 and it's the oldest black parade in New Orleans. Louis Armstrong, the famous jazz musician, was once the king of Zulu. The members dress in African costumes and paint their faces black. They wear grass skirts, wigs, and scary masks while they dance and give painted coconuts to the crowds."

"But if they are already black, why do they paint their faces black?"

"The krewe members paint their faces black as a joke," Mom laughed. "When you grow up you'll see how lucky you were to ride in the Zulu parade."

My mom says I worry too much, but sometimes I just like to think about things.

The next week, Mom brought me to meet the queen and the other pages. We had to take pictures for the newspaper.

Queen Simms was very nice and said, "D.J., this is Leah and Saia, my two girl pages, and this is Brandon, my other boy page. All of you are seven except Saia, who's six years old."

Leah said, "Queen Simms is my grandmother and my mother is a lady in waiting and she's going to ride on the float with us."

While we played, Mom made the arrangements about my costume, which means she got all the details. Mrs. Simms was representing an Egyptian queen. We didn't have to paint our faces black, but we did have to wear wigs. Our costumes were red and gold tunics decorated with sequins.

When the photographer was ready, Mom complained that my shirt was out of my pants and I had lost my tie. She said that I was sweaty too. (Mom hates for me to sweat in my suit.)

"I found your tie and it's dirty," Saia snickered as she held it up like a worm.

"Thank you, Saia," Mom said as she dusted it off and gave me one of her "why-don't-you-listen" stares.

The photographer took a lot of photos until Mom was pleased. She told the photographer that the last one was cute.

I hate taking pictures . . . especially when Mom's around.

Mom and Dad kept telling everyone they talked to about me being a page in the parade. I didn't tell anyone except Eddie, my best friend at school.

One evening after karate practice, Mom brought me to Mrs. Hardesty, the dressmaker, to get fitted for my costume.

"You are the last little page to come here," Mrs. Hardesty said with a smile. She slipped the red and gold costume over my head. "Your costume is a perfect fit."

Mrs. Hardesty showed me a picture of how my costume should look when it was finished. We were going to look like Egyptian warriors. I liked my costume and I liked Mrs. Hardesty.

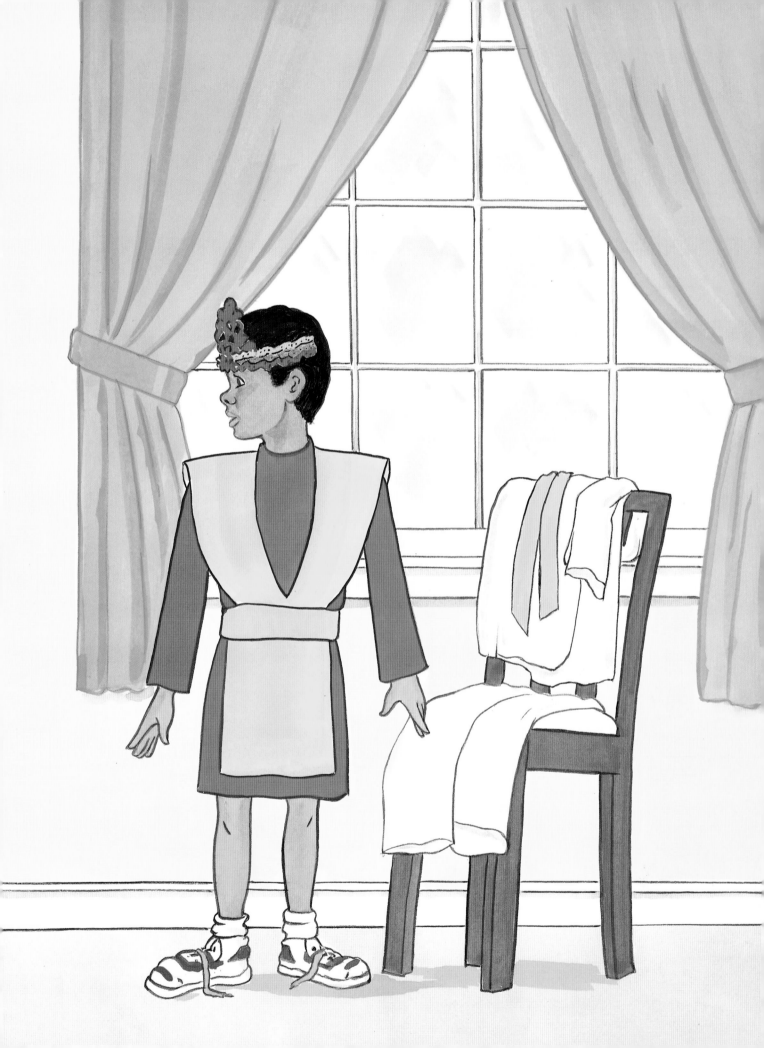

Dad brought home a big box one day and told me to open it. When I did, guess what was in it? Beads, beads, and more beads! Four hundred gross, I think, at least that's what Dad said. The only problem was that all the beads were the same size and color. They were all black, with an oval medallion and a gold letter *Z* on top.

"Is this all that I will throw?" I asked Dad. "What about toys, spears, and stuffed animals? Don't I get any of those?"

"I'm afraid not, D.J., because on the queen's float you can only throw Club Zulu's official beads," said Dad. "But son, that's an awful lot of beads for a small boy like you to throw."

Later that evening, my sisters sorted all my beads and put them in a blue duffel bag.

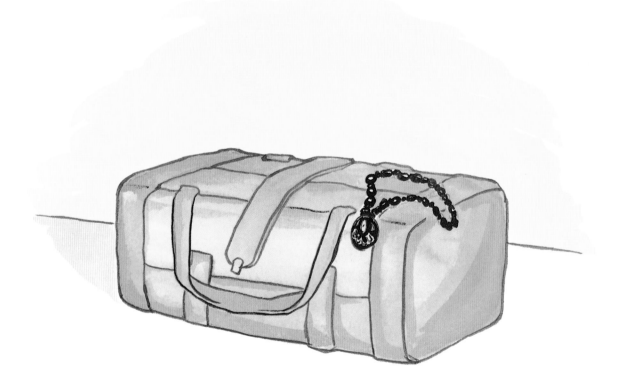

The night before the parade, my costume was laid out on the chair next to my bed. Mom said we had to get up early to meet Queen Zulu at the hotel.

"D.J.," said Mom, "I bought you some thermal underwear in case the weather gets cold."

"My stomach hurts, Mom." (It didn't really hurt. It just felt funny inside.)

"Oh, you just have butterflies in your tummy. How about some warm milk?" Mom asked.

"How do butterflies get in your stomach?" I asked Mom worriedly.

"There aren't real butterflies in your stomach. Sometimes our stomachs get a jumpy feeling inside, when we're worried about something," said Mom. "D.J., are you worried about the parade tomorrow?"

"Well, kind of," I whispered. "I mean, what if I fell off the float . . . who would catch me?"

"Your dad talked to the parade captain and was told that everyone is required to wear a harness securing them to the float," said Mom reassuringly.

"But Mom, what if the harness breaks? And what if I have to use the bathroom? And everyone keeps telling me to throw them something, but, what if I don't see them?"

"D.J., your dad and I are riding in a limousine behind your float. If anything happens we will be right there. Try not to worry so much. Everything will be fine. You'll have a great day! Would you like me to read you a bedtime story to help you fall asleep?"

Mom fell asleep before I did.

Mom says I worry too much, but sometimes I just have to think about things.

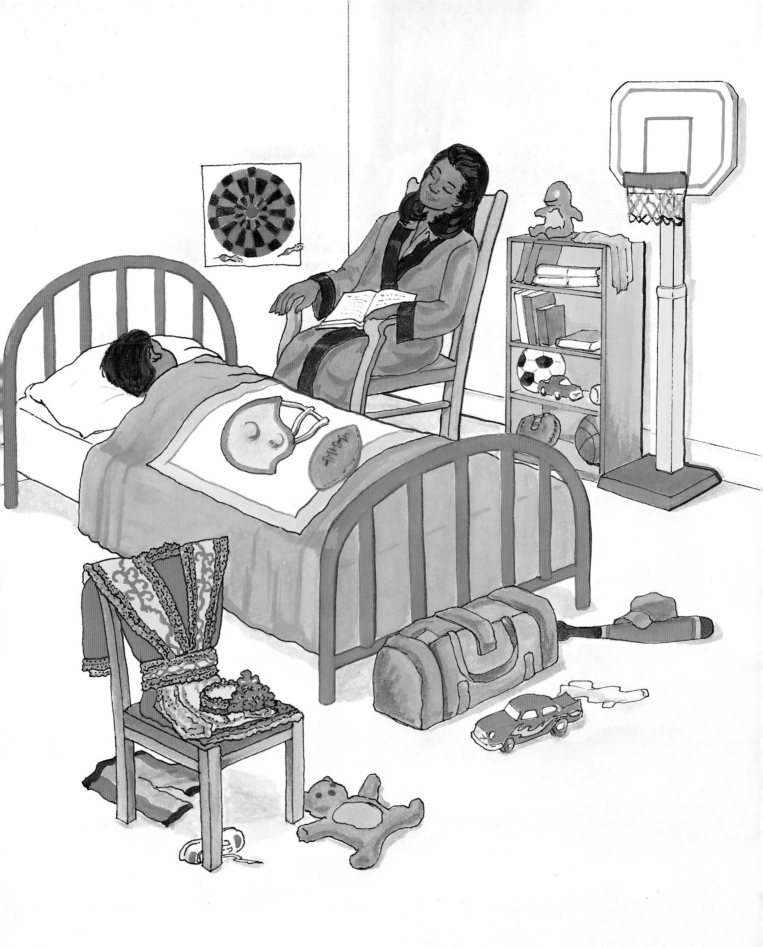

When I woke up the next morning, I was already dressed. Sometimes Mom does that—dresses me while I'm sleeping.

"Good morning, sleepyhead," Mom said cheerfully. "How about some chocolate doughnuts and milk for breakfast?"

Dad had my toothbrush waiting and everything was already loaded in the car.

We left home at six in the morning and there were many cars on the street.

"Why is traffic so heavy this early in the morning?" I asked.

"Because it's Mardi Gras Day and people leave home early to get a good spot along the parade route," said Dad. "Most people pack picnic lunches and spend the whole day in one spot, like we did last year."

"Wow, look at all those big floats!" I exclaimed. "Am I riding on that one? Look at all the people in African costumes!"

"The king and queen's floats are over there," said Dad. "Each float has a different theme. This one is called the Witch Doctor float, over there is Big Shot, and there's the Snake Charmer. The Zulu parade has many colorful floats, marching groups, and bands. It's noted for traditions, like giving out coconuts to the crowds and not following the parade route."

I watched as the krewe members carried all of their throws onto each float. They loaded toy spears, beads, plastic cups, and miniature umbrellas. Then they carefully loaded large sacks of gold-and-black-painted coconuts.

This might be fun after all.

On our way to the hotel room, I could hear the music of the bands warming up for the parade. When we entered Mrs. Simms' room she was dressed in a red and gold sequined gown with an enormous feathered collar with snake designs on it. Saia, Brandon, and Leah were all dressed like me. I couldn't tell them apart.

Leah's mother told me, "D.J., come here and let me put on your makeup and your lipstick."

"Lipstick," I echoed. The other pages started giggling. *"Lipstick!"* I screamed. "No way, not me." I hid behind the nearest door. I went along with the stockings and the wig but this was the last straw.

"Come on, D.J.," Mom pleaded. "Please cooperate. It's just for one day."

Mom brought me over to Leah's mother, even though I made the meanest face that I could. I put my lips together tightly and squinted my eyes. No one told me that I had to wear lipstick!

We rode in a limousine to the queen's float. The queen's float was almost two stories high. We had to climb a ladder to get to the top. Our parents secured us to the harnesses and hung our beads on the hooks that were provided.

The view from the top of our float was great. I could even see my favorite band, the St. Augustine marching band. When I grow up I'm going to that high school, because my dad and uncles went there.

The king of Zulu's float was before ours and his outfit was enormous. His costume was pink and maroon with gold coconuts and plumes all around his collar.

As the float started moving, my heart was beating fast. What if I fall off this float? My sisters said that last year someone fell off a float.

The other pages started throwing beads. Saia was throwing handfuls at one time.

"You're not supposed to throw so much at a time," I tried to tell her, "or you will run out before the parade is over." But she wouldn't listen.

The crowds were spread out from the street to the houses. I've never seen so many people at one time, all yelling, "Throw me something, mister!"

I thought I heard my name a couple of times, but I did not look down in case I would fall.

I threw beads mostly to children on ladders and people on balconies.

Somebody had to think about them.

Our float stopped at Gallier Hall, so that the mayor could toast the king and queen of Zulu. I waved at the mayor.

"When I grow up I want to be the mayor," I told Brandon.

"Why would you want to be the mayor?" laughed Brandon.

"So that I could be in charge of the firemen and policemen," I said.

Just then I heard Mom's voice calling my name. "D.J., would you kids like some candy?" Everyone else started screaming yes, but I was going to say no in case we got in trouble with the queen. Mom handed me a bag full of candy. Brandon ate so much his lipstick came off.

"See that man over there?" giggled Leah. "He's dressed like a dinosaur. And that boy over there is wearing a football uniform."

After that we started pointing out different or unusual costumes. We saw babies dressed like bunnies, and people masked as cowboys, Indians, and Gypsies. But what we saw most were clowns wearing the funniest costumes.

When Saia got tired and ran out of beads to throw, she made her parents take her off the float. The rest of us watched the crowds and tried to spot the funniest costumes. Every time St. Aug's band played, we danced on the float.

Our ride ended at Armstrong Park. Then we boarded a bus back to the hotel. The queen had drinks and snacks waiting for us. She thanked us and said that we were lovely pages and she was glad she picked us to ride with her.

Mom leaned over and whispered to me, "Weren't you a lucky boy to ride in the Zulu parade?"

"Yes," I whispered back, "it was a lot of fun."